drug facts
ALCOHOL

TED GOTTFRIED with Katherine Follett

Marshall Cavendish
Benchmark
New York

Marshall Cavendish Benchmark
99 White Plains Road
Tarrytown, NY 10591
www.marshallcavendish.us

Library of Congress Cataloging-in-Publication Data

Gottfried, Ted.
    Alcohol / by Ted Gottfried with Katherine Follett.
        p. cm. — (Benchmark rockets : drug facts)
    Includes index.
    Summary: "Discusses the history, effects, and dangers of alcohol as well as addiction treatment options"—Provided by publisher.
        ISBN 978-0-7614-4348-3
1. Alcoholism—Juvenile literature. 2. Alcohol—Physiological effect—Juvenile literature. 3. Drinking of alcoholic beverages—Juvenile literature. I. Follett, Katherine. II. Title.

HV5066.G68 2010
613.81—dc22
2008052751

Publisher: Michelle Bisson
Editorial Development and Book Design: Trillium Publishing, Inc.

Photo research by Trillium Publishing, Inc.

Cover photo: Ctacik/Dreamstime.com

The photographs and illustrations in this book are used by permission and through the courtesy of: *Shutterstock.com*: Jose AS Reyes, 1; 6; Galina Barskaya, 22. *iStockphoto.com*: Alex Brosa, 4; pixhook, 8; László Rákoskerti, 19; ericsphotography, 25. *Library of Congress*: 10, 12 (portrait), 14. *Getty Images*: American Stock/Hulton Archive, 12 (cartoon). *Jupiterimages Corporation*: 17.

Printed in Malaysia
1 3 5 6 4 2

CONTENTS

1 Alcohol and You

DRINKING ALCOHOL CAN BE FUN. IT CAN ALSO LEAD TO tragedy. One drink might make a person feel good. Frequent drinking might lead to **alcoholism**. Drinking might make you feel cheerful, or it might make you feel sad or sick or act in a mean manner. The way a person responds to alcohol depends on many things. These things include age, sex, weight, genes, mood, and the amount of alcohol that a person drinks.

Should you have a drink when you're over 21? Will one drink lead to another? Will you drink at every party? When you're not at parties, will you drink? Will you develop a drinking problem? The answers to these questions are not the same for everyone. This book will give you the facts you need to answer these questions for yourself.

Young adults have to make decisions about drinking.

How Alcohol Affects the Body

When you drink beer, wine, **liquor**, or other beverages that are made with alcohol, the alcohol goes to your stomach first. From the stomach, it's absorbed into your bloodstream. If you have food in your stomach, then the alcohol is absorbed more slowly. If you mix alcohol with a sparkling drink, like soda, then the alcohol is absorbed more quickly. It's also absorbed more quickly if your drink has more than one kind of alcohol in it. The more quickly the alcohol is absorbed, the faster you will get drunk.

After the alcohol is absorbed into your blood, it travels quickly to your brain. Your brain controls your thoughts, emotions, and movement. Alcohol affects these things.

Alcohol acts as a **depressant** on the brain. At first, the alcohol may give you a jolt of excitement and energy. Overall, however, your thoughts, emotions, and movements will relax or slow down. You might feel relaxed right after drinking. The rules that you have for yourself might relax as well. You might do or say things that you wouldn't normally do or say and feel more friendly and enthusiastic than before.

Then, when the jolt of energy wears off, your thoughts, speech, and reflexes begin to slow down. You might feel tired, weak, confused, or sick.

More drinks will increase the effects of alcohol. So will drinking faster.

How Alcohol Affects the Body

Stomach: Alcohol goes straight to the stomach. From the stomach, it gets absorbed into the bloodstream. Having food in the stomach will slow down this process.

Bloodstream: Alcohol in the bloodstream flows throughout the body and to the brain.

Brain: Alcohol is a depressant, which means it slows down communication in the brain and between the brain and body. Reflexes become slower. Rules seem looser. A person may become clumsy or even pass out.

Liver: The liver filters alcohol out of the bloodstream and breaks it down. Over time, alcohol can damage the liver.

Bladder: After the body processes the alcohol, it's passed as urine. Alcohol causes people to urinate more, which can lead to too much water loss. Losing too much water makes people sick and contributes to hangovers.

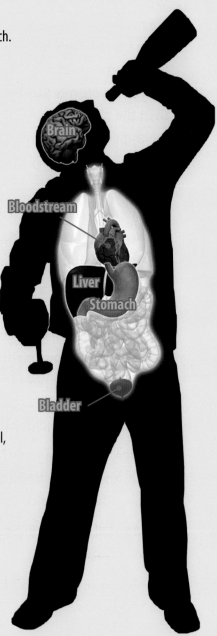

Eventually, your body will process the alcohol, and the immediate effects go away. But there are long-term effects that do not go away.

Abuse and Addiction

People who drink heavily or often are in danger of abusing alcohol. Over time, the body becomes used to alcohol's effects. So the drinker needs to drink more alcohol in order to feel the same effects. Alcohol is also **addictive**. After time, the body needs alcohol, and the drinker feels terrible without it.

Alcohol addiction is called alcoholism. Alcoholism can harm many parts of the body. Heavy drinking can damage the mouth, **esophagus**, and stomach. **Cirrhosis**—a disease of the liver—is common in people suffering from alcoholism.

People who suffer from alcoholism are called **alcoholics**. When alcoholics try to stop drinking, things usually get worse before they get better. Alcoholics might suffer terrible **hallucinations** and shaking that can kill them. But if they don't stop drinking, they may die from alcoholism. Alcoholism can cause other losses, too, such as broken relationships, lost jobs, and lost dreams.

Will Alcohol Be a Problem for Me?

The majority of American adults have an occasional drink. But not everyone who drinks develops a drinking problem. When does regular drinking become a problem, and why?

Some people are more at risk for alcoholism than others. For one thing, the younger a person starts drinking, the more likely he or she is to develop a serious drinking problem. People who start drinking before they are 15 years old are four times more likely to become alcoholics than people who start drinking when they are 21 or older.

Young adults and alcohol are a combination that can have other dangerous consequences. There is a link between alcohol use and a high suicide rate among teenagers. **Binge drinking**, or drinking enough to become ill or pass out, can result in hospitalization, date rapes, unwanted pregnancies, and even death. Young drinkers are more at risk of serious or deadly car accidents than older drinkers are. Young drinkers are also breaking the law and can face strict punishment.

This may paint a dark picture of alcohol, but there's another side. Many adults drink and are not alcoholics. And research shows that a **moderate** amount of alcohol can actually have positive effects on an adult body. A moderate amount of alcohol is defined as one to two drinks a day.

One drink equals one serving of alcohol. Some drinks have more alcohol in them than other drinks. So "one drink" isn't always the same size.

12 ounces
(355 milliliters)
of beer

5 ounces
(148 ml)
of wine

1.5 ounces
(44 ml)
of liquor

Health Benefits for Adults

People in countries like France and Italy have fewer heart attacks than people in the United States. Research shows that the love of red wine in these countries helps keep the people's hearts healthy.

Some studies show that it's not just wine that keeps hearts healthy. These studies suggest that moderate amounts of any alcohol taken regularly—for example, with dinner—can help the heart.

An American study looked at the effects of moderate alcohol use in adult men. The study found that men who had two drinks a day, three or four days a week, had 68 percent less risk for heart attacks than men who drank less. Another study showed a similar effect in adult women.

It's important to remember that drinking large amounts of alcohol—for example, drinking six beers on a Saturday night—has many more health risks than benefits. It's also important to remember that all of these studies were done only with adults.

Adults' brains, bodies, and emotional systems are fully developed, which isn't true for young people. In addition, the risk of a young person having a heart attack is very small. These two facts make the dangers for young drinkers greatly outweigh the benefits. And the dangers are clear—in one recent survey, young drinkers had death rates twice as high as young nondrinkers.

When making a decision about alcohol, it is important to look at both the benefits and the risks.

The History of Alcohol

ALCOHOL BEGAN AS AN ACCIDENT MORE THAN TEN thousand years ago. A sugary fruit, maybe grapes, was heated up enough for **fermentation** to occur. Early humans tasted the fermented fruit and liked the taste and the pleasant feeling it gave them. They probably didn't like the **hangover** that followed! They began fermenting fruit on purpose, and people have been drinking beer and wine ever since. Thousands of years later, people started making and drinking liquor.

The Women's Christian Temperance Union prayed at bars to try to get the people there to stop drinking.

A Drinking Nation

Alcohol has been a part of U.S. history from the very start. When Europeans began to settle in the United States in the 1600s, they brought alcohol with them. They brought over gin and made their own beer and cider. Many of these people were **Puritans**. Puritans thought of alcohol as the "Good Creature of God" and believed it improved health in many ways. But they did not like drunkenness. Only people who would not get drunk were allowed to drink in bars.

By the early 1800s, the average American drank about 7 gallons of alcohol per year. That's nearly 180 glasses of wine or six hundred servings of liquor!

Not all Americans saw good in alcohol, especially in such large amounts. Many religious groups thought alcohol led to health problems, laziness, and sin. They tried to get people to stop drinking. Their efforts worked. Between 1825 and 1840, the amount that Americans drank was cut in half. This changed as more and more German and Irish settlers arrived. Beer and whiskey were part of their culture.

Religious groups continued working to stop people from drinking. In 1851, the state of Maine made it illegal to sell alcohol. In 1873, the Woman's Christian **Temperance** Union (WCTU) began sitting in bars and praying. WCTU members would return to a bar day after day until the bar was forced to close. Anti-alcohol efforts were becoming more popular.

The Start of Prohibition

The biggest support for the WCTU came from the wives of working men. They were hurt badly by alcohol abuse, and their children were, too. Their husbands spent so much money on liquor that there was hardly any cash left for food or clothing. Depressed and frustrated working men often got

Carry Nation

If you spoke about the WCTU around 1900, most people would picture Carry Nation. They would see a 6-foot (2-meter) tall woman, with arm muscles bulging under her black and white dress.

Nation would burst into a bar carrying an ax. She'd start swinging her ax wildly—breaking bottles, smashing kegs, and destroying mirrors and windows—while yelling at the people in the bar that she had come to save them from their fate.

She destroyed bars in New York, Washington, Pittsburgh, and San Francisco. She was arrested more than 30 times.

People laughed about Nation's wild ways. Yet no one could deny that she brought a lot of attention to the anti-alcohol movement.

drunk, and sometimes they took out their frustrations on their wives and children.

Some people made fun of the WCTU for being so serious. But the WCTU's concerns about the bad effects of alcohol were real.

By 1913, more than half the states had laws about alcohol use, but that wasn't enough for the WCTU. The WCTU and others wanted the government to pass anti-alcohol laws for the whole country. That happened in 1919, when a new amendment was added to the U.S. Constitution. The Eighteenth Amendment made it illegal to make or sell alcohol in the United States. The period known as **Prohibition** began.

Speakeasies, Bathtub Brews, and Mobsters

Even during Prohibition, alcohol was never too hard to find. It was especially easy to get alcohol in the nation's big cities. In New York City, 15,000 bars were closed. But 32,000 **speakeasies** replaced them. Speakeasies were places where illegal alcohol was served. People drank the alcohol from teacups or soup bowls to disguise it.

People got illegal alcohol in one of two ways: they made it, or they snuck it in from other countries. Gin was especially easy to make at home, in homemade setups called stills, or in bathtubs. Homemade liquor often tasted terrible, so people mixed it with fruit juices or sodas. Many mixed drinks, such as the Bloody Mary, were invented during this time and are still popular today.

Mobsters like Al Capone brought illegal alcohol into the United States from Canada and other countries. Capone and others made a lot of money from this illegal business. Mobsters got rich enough to pay for the campaigns of politicians that they liked and to bribe politicians. Mob wars, murders, and other acts of violence became common as a result of the money involved in this business. There were shoot-outs, and innocent people were sometimes killed.

Many Americans became frustrated with the law because it did not work, and it caused so much violence. Eventually, the Constitution was changed again. In 1933, another amendment was added. The Twenty-First Amendment did away with the Eighteenth Amendment. Alcohol was legal again.

A Scientist's Viewpoint

Like many, famous scientist Albert Einstein was frustrated by Prohibition. Einstein said that "nothing is more disruptive of respect for the government and the law of the land than passing laws which can't be enforced." He blamed the Eighteenth Amendment for "the dangerous increase of crime in this country."

Many people saw Prohibition as a failure. But it did reduce some problems with alcohol. The number of hospital trips caused by drinking dropped. So did the number of alcohol-related deaths.

Today's Laws

Today, there are still laws about alcohol use. One of the strongest laws about alcohol in the United States is about the minimum drinking age.

For a long time, different states had different ages at which people could drink. In 1984, it became illegal in all states to sell alcohol to anyone under 21 years old. Supporters point out that this law has reduced deaths from underage drunk drivers by 43 percent. But not everyone supports this law. Some say it's easy to get around it by using a fake identification card.

Another strong U.S. law about alcohol use is the law against drinking and driving. This law became stricter in the early 1980s, after 20-year-old Joe Tursi was killed by a drunk driver. The driver's punishment was only four years of **probation** and a small fine. Joe's mother was outraged. She formed Mothers Against Drunk Driving (MADD) and began working for stricter laws against drunk driving.

MADD helped pass a new national law about drinking and driving in 2000. Before this law, states made up their own laws about drinking and driving. In some states, it was legal to drive with a blood alcohol content (BAC) level of up to 0.10 percent. The BAC level is used to measure how drunk a person is. The new law made it illegal to drive with a BAC level higher than 0.08 percent—anywhere in the country.

A BAC level is the result of many things, including how much a person weighs, what he or she drank, how much he or she drank, and the amount of food in his or her stomach. There are BAC calculators on the Internet that can help people estimate their BACs, but these estimates are often wrong. It's best to simply not drive after drinking.

The U.S. government controls alcohol in another way. They tax it. Alcohol taxes make alcohol more expensive. This reduces the amount people drink. Alcohol taxes also bring in money that the government can use for health care, education, and programs that treat alcohol abuse.

Timeline of Alcohol Laws

1851　Maine makes it illegal to make or sell alcohol.

1873　Woman's Christian Temperance Union (WCTU) forms.

1919　The Eighteenth Amendment to the Constitution makes it illegal to make or sell alcohol.

1933　The Twenty-First Amendment to the Constitution makes it legal to make and sell alcohol again.

1980　Mothers Against Drunk Driving (MADD) forms.

1984　The National Minimum Drinking Age Act makes it illegal to sell alcohol to anyone under 21 in the United States.

2000　President Bill Clinton signs a new national law that makes it illegal to drive with a BAC level higher than 0.08 percent.

The history of alcohol in America and the changing laws reflect just how hard it is to make the right choices about drinking.

3 Recognizing a Drinking Problem

THERE ARE MORE THAN 3 MILLION TEENAGE ALCOHOLICS in the United States. Several million other teens may have serious drinking problems that require help. Alcohol abuse is linked to emotional and behavioral problems. It also contributes to car crashes, suicides, and murders—the three leading causes of death for young people.

Not everyone who drinks becomes an alcoholic. But more than 20 million people in the United States have a serious problem with alcohol. Why do some people drink without a problem, while others become alcoholics? What does a drinking problem look like? And what should you do if you or a loved one has a problem with alcohol?

It's not always easy to talk to a family member about his or her drinking problem. Often, it's a good idea to get help from someone outside the family.

Alcoholism: A Problem in the Family

Many people have noticed that alcoholism runs in families. The child of an alcoholic is four times more likely to develop alcoholism than someone who does not have alcoholism in the family. This has led people to believe that alcoholism may be in a person's **genes**.

Genes are passed down from parents to children. They affect the way a person looks and his or her risk of getting certain diseases. Genes are also thought to play a role in the way a person feels or acts. For example, someone's genes may make it likely that he or she will become depressed. Genes may also make it likely that someone will become addicted to drugs or alcohol.

If it's true that alcoholism is in some people's genes, then alcoholism can be thought of as a disease. There is some comfort and hope in this view of alcoholism. No one blames the victim of a disease for his or her sickness, and many diseases have cures. The view that alcoholism is a disease therefore suggests that alcoholics should not be blamed for having a problem with alcohol.

While it's clear that alcoholism runs in families, not everyone agrees that the reason for this is genetic. Another idea is that children who grow up around alcoholism see their role models drink regularly. This might make drinking seem normal. Children who are raised by alcoholics may not be able to recognize the signs of a drinking problem in themselves— at least not before it's too late.

If You Have a Drinking Problem

It's important to recognize a drinking problem before it gets dangerous. So where is the line between drinking and a drinking problem?

If you have a drinking problem, alcohol can create problems in your life. You may start getting bad grades or doing poorly at work. You may get into trouble while drinking. You may get violent, have risky sex, or fight with friends and family while drunk. A drinking problem becomes alcoholism when the body and mind *need* alcohol. An alcoholic can't function without drinking.

If you think you have a drinking problem, then it's important to get help. Ideally, it's best to talk to your parents first, but, for many reasons, this might be difficult. If you can't talk to your parents, look for a school counselor or social worker. These people will not judge you. They will not be emotionally involved in your problem, either. This might make it easier for them to help you than it would be for a family member to do so.

Drinking can make people feel alone. If you think you might have a problem with alcohol, then it's important to reach out to someone you trust.

Are You an Alcoholic?

A Simple 12-Question Quiz
to Help You Decide

1. Do you drink because you have problems or to deal with stressful situations?

2. Do you drink when you get mad at other people?

3. Do you think it's cool to be able to hold your liquor?

4. Do you prefer to drink alone, rather than with others?

5. Are you starting to get low grades? Are you goofing off at school or work?

6. Do you ever try to stop drinking or to drink less—and fail?

7. Do you drink in the morning, before school or work?

8. Do you gulp your drinks as if to satisfy a great thirst?

9. Do you ever have a loss of memory due to your drinking?

10. Do you lie about your drinking?

11. Do you ever get into trouble when you are drinking?

12. Do you often get drunk when you drink, even when you don't mean to?

If you can answer "yes" to any of these questions, it's time you took a serious look at what your drinking might be doing to you.

If Your Parent Has a Drinking Problem

Young people who never drink can still have a problem with alcohol. This is because if someone you love has a drinking problem, that problem affects you, too.

Nearly 27 million children have an alcoholic parent. Children of alcoholics may not admit that their parent has a problem. Some may blame themselves for their parent's drinking. They may think, "If only I had cleaned my room or come home on time, then Mom or Dad would not have gotten drunk."

No child is to blame for a parent's alcoholism. No child can stop a parent from drinking. So, what can a young person do if Mom or Dad is an alcoholic?

If your parent is an alcoholic, first find an adult you can trust and talk to. It can be another family member, a teacher, someone in your religious community, or a school counselor. If you don't feel comfortable with someone you know, contact Alateen, a group that helps teenagers who have alcoholic loved ones.

After you talk to someone about your parent's problem, use the following advice to help yourself, until your parent gets the help that he or she needs.

- Don't try to stop your parent from drinking by throwing away or hiding the alcohol. This could make him or her angry and only starts a fight.

- If your parent is violent, don't try to fight with him or her. Instead, get away, and call the police. It may feel terrible to call the police on your parent, but things could get much worse if the violence isn't stopped.

- If your parent drives drunk with you in the car, you need to call for help. It's dangerous and against the law for anyone to drive while drunk. To report a drunk driver, call 911 or 800-28-DRUNK.

- Try not to make your parent's drinking the focus of your life. Involve yourself in activities outside the home, such as sports, clubs, or groups. You should not be embarrassed about talking it over with your friends. True friends can be just the support you need.

During hard times, friends can be a great support.

Other Loved Ones Who Drink

It's not easy to deal with a sister or brother who has a drinking problem, either. If your brother or sister is older than you, he or she may ignore your concerns just because you are younger. On the other hand, if your brother or sister is younger than you, he or she might not like having an older sibling trying to step in, and he or she may get annoyed with you for doing so. In either case, it's best to get help from a trusted adult.

It's also hard to deal with a friend who has a drinking problem. You may want to help, but you also don't want to make your friend mad. Your friend may not admit to having a problem. Or he or she might try to defend himself or herself. Sometimes, the best thing to do is to be there if and when your friend wants to talk. However, if your friend is doing something dangerous, such as breaking the law, having unprotected sex, or talking about suicide, then it's time to involve an adult. You may lose a friend, but you may also save a life.

4 Help, Hope, and Healing

IF YOU OR A LOVED ONE HAS A PROBLEM WITH ALCOHOL, there is hope. There are many organizations that help alcoholics and their loved ones.

Alcoholics Anonymous

Alcoholics Anonymous (AA) is the most well-known treatment program. It's a nationwide organization, made up of small groups of people who meet regularly to talk about alcoholism and to support each other. Membership is free. All that is required is the desire to stop drinking.

At AA meetings, people go by their first names only. They speak freely about their experiences with alcohol, knowing that other alcoholics will understand. AA sees alcoholism as a disease. According to this view, an alcoholic can't control his or her drinking. The only way to control alcoholism is to stop drinking entirely. Members of AA follow 12 steps to stop drinking. AA sees the treatment of alcoholism as a lifelong process.

AA estimates that it has 2 million members. It has become the alcohol treatment program that the government, courts, businesses, and religious groups send people to for help.

There are support groups for people recovering from the effects of living with an alcoholic.

Al-Anon and Alateen

Many other addiction groups have used AA's beliefs and methods. Two of these groups are Al-Anon and Alateen.

Al-Anon helps people deal with the alcoholism of a friend or family member. There are over 24,000 Al-Anon groups in 115 countries.

Alateen is a branch of Al-Anon. Alateen helps only young people. Group members come together to talk about their experiences and offer support as they learn to cope with the alcoholism of their loved ones. Members of Alateen learn that alcoholism is a disease they did not cause and can't cure. There are over 2,300 Alateen groups worldwide.

Alternatives to AA

Other treatment programs treat alcoholism in different ways. For example, Drinkwatchers sees alcoholism as a behavior rather than a disease. It uses a method of praise and rewards to encourage people to limit drinking.

Some programs help certain groups of people, such as Women for Sobriety (WFS). In the early days of AA, many AA members wrongly believed that women could not be alcoholics. Women were not allowed to join AA and were treated rudely. WFS was created to help women worldwide recover from alcoholism. Since 1976, WFS has supported women alcoholics by offering self-help groups and encouraging positive thinking, meditation, and good nutrition.

In Chicago, there is a recovery group just for police officers. It recognizes that many police officers turn to alcohol to deal with the stress and danger of their jobs. Other programs work with pregnant women who have drinking problems. These women put their unborn children at risk of **fetal alcohol syndrome**, which can cause brain damage and health problems. There are also groups for veterans, medical workers, former prisoners, and others.

Help for alcoholics or problem drinkers can come from many places and in many different forms, but most treatment programs agree that the person seeking treatment must truly want to deal with his or her problem with alcohol. The first step to recovery for a person who struggles with alcohol is to admit that there is a problem.

Hope

There is a lot of hope for people who have a problem with alcohol. Alcoholics and their loved ones must be open to anything that will help make their lives better. Whether alcoholism comes from a person's genes, behavior, or a combination of the two, what is most important is to recover from the problem.

One of the most powerful things to remember, if you or a loved one has an alcohol problem, is that you are not alone. Millions of people around the world have dealt with alcohol abuse and addiction. And millions have successfully traveled down the road of recovery.

Talking to someone, whether publicly or privately, can give an alcoholic support and hope. Talking with other alcoholics can provide understanding and a model for recovery.

We may never solve all the problems of alcoholism. But we can reach out and help those who want to change.

GLOSSARY

addictive: Something that causes a state in which a person's body and mind are unable to give up something, like a drug or a habit.

alcoholism: A long-lasting and uncontrollable need for alcohol.

alcoholics: People who have a long-lasting and uncontrollable need for alcohol.

binge drinking: Drinking five or more drinks that have alcohol in them at a single sitting, or drinking enough to become severely drunk.

cirrhosis: A disease of the liver in which healthy liver tissue is replaced by scar tissue, common among long-term alcoholics.

depressant: Having the effect of slowing down the brain and its functions.

esophagus: The tube that connects the back of the mouth to the stomach.

fermentation: The process in which yeast changes sugar into alcohol and carbon dioxide.

fetal alcohol syndrome: A group of health problems that a baby is born with as a result of the baby's mother drinking alcohol during her pregnancy.

genes: The parts of cells that pass physical and behavioral traits from parent to child.

hallucinations: Experiences in which a person believes that imaginary sights, sounds, tastes, smells, or feelings are real.

hangover: Flu-like symptoms that occur after heavy drinking.

liquor: A strong beverage—such as vodka, whiskey, or tequila—that is made by heating up a liquid until it sends off a vapor, or gas, and then cooling the gas back into a liquid. This process is called distillation.

mobsters: Members of criminal gangs.

moderate: Neither very much nor very little.

probation: A punishment for a crime in which a person is watched for a period of time to make sure he or she does not commit another crime.

Prohibition: The time during which alcohol was illegal in the United States (from 1920 to 1933).

Puritans: Strict followers of the English Protestant Church, in the 1700–1800s.

speakeasies: Illegal clubs disguised as something other than bars, where alcohol was served during Prohibition.

temperance: The habit of not drinking much or any alcohol.

FIND OUT MORE

Books

Aretha, David. *On the Rocks: Teens and Alcohol*. New York: Franklin Watts, 2007.

Gottfried, Ted. *The Facts about Alcohol*. New York: Marshall Cavendish, 2005.

Hornik-Beer, Edith. *For Teenagers Living with a Parent Who Abuses Alcohol/Drugs*. Lincoln, NE: iUniverse.com, 2001.

McClellan, Marilyn. *The Big Deal About Alcohol: What Teens Need to Know About Drinking*. New York: Enslow, 2004.

Nakaya, Andrea C. *Alcohol (Opposing Viewpoints)*. New York: Greenhaven, 2007.

Shannon, Joyce Brennfleck. *Alcohol Information for Teens: Health Tips about Alcohol and Alcoholism*. Danbury, CT: Omnigraphics, 2004.

Websites

Al-Anon/Alateen
http://www.al-anon.alateen.org

Alcoholics Anonymous
http://www.aa.org

Check Yourself: A Place for Teens to Check Where They Are With Drugs and Alcohol
http://www.checkyourself.com

Mothers Against Drunk Driving (MADD)
http://www.madd.org

National Association for Children of Alcoholics (NACoA)
http://www.nacoa.net

INDEX

Page numbers for photographs and illustrations are in **boldface**.